THE AIRPORT

The Inside Story

NEON  SQUID

Contents

Welcome to the airport!

Hello! My name is John Walton, and I am an aviation journalist. That means I write articles, make podcasts, and appear on television—all talking about airplanes and how we travel.

I love airports! I took my first flight when I was just eight weeks old, because I was born in a different country than the one my parents came from and they wanted me to meet the rest of my family. As I grew up living in many different countries, I went to airports very often—to visit family and friends, to travel on vacation, or just to watch the planes.

When I was your age, I also loved reading about airports. And even as a grown-up, I still do! Airports are unlike any other place in the world. A lot of people work very hard at different jobs to make sure our journeys are smooth from the moment we set foot in the airport. We count on all sorts of people to check our luggage, get us to the plane, fly us high up in the sky, and make sure we're safe throughout our trip.

There are a lot of really fun things about airports, but sometimes they can be a little confusing. After all, we don't go to airports every single day… unless we work there! If you ever feel worried or concerned, remember that there are people who work at the airport who are there to help.

Learning about airports and the people who work there—and all the people who travel through them—is really fascinating. I hope you enjoy it as much as I do! If you're traveling through an airport soon, see if you can spot all the different staff doing their particular jobs. Keep an eye out for the special vehicles too, and of course, my favorite: the airplanes.

Happy travels!

John Walton

Getting to the airport

Sofia's grandpa drops her, her parents, and her brother Rohan off at the airport in his car. Sofia and Rohan are very excited! Their family is visiting relatives who live far away, so they have a lot of luggage. Before leaving the house this morning, their dad checked off items on a list to make sure that everyone had everything they needed for their trip: "Toothpaste—check! Passport—check! Underwear—check!"

Melinda and her dads arrive by train at the station underneath the airport. She enjoyed the fast train whizzing along the tracks at top speed. The family are going on their first vacation abroad. Melinda insists on pulling her brand-new suitcase all the way to the airplane. This is going to be her first time flying. She's a little bit nervous, but her dads reassure her that it's going to be fun!

Priya wheels herself off the bus and into the terminal. She is flying to a business meeting at her company's headquarters. Priya flies all over the world for her job, but she has never been to this airport before. She can't wait to look around and browse the shops before boarding.

Checking in

Check-in is the first place you go when you get to the airport. It's a big, busy hall with lots of desks where check-in agents like Paul make sure you and your luggage get onto the right airplane. They also help you reserve your seats if you haven't already. First, Paul checks everybody's passport. Sofia's mom has them all in a small folder so that they don't get lost. Paul then prints out boarding passes for everyone. These are special tickets that have to be presented before passengers board the plane.

Tasha picks up her boarding pass from the self check-in machine.

The family's bigger bags have to go into the luggage area of the airplane, which is called the hold. Paul uses a computer to print a tag that says where the bag is going and whom it belongs to. He sticks the tag to the bag's handle, and—*whoosh*—off it goes down the baggage belt.

While Sofia's family is almost done checking in, Tasha has just arrived without a suitcase and is using a self check-in machine to print her boarding pass. A few quick taps on the screen and she's ready to go!

Check-in agents can also help passengers with any last-minute flight changes.

Malu tells Rohan to walk through.

The X-ray machine

Sofia and Rohan's family arrives at the security area. This is the part of the airport where staff check to make sure that passengers have nothing forbidden in their luggage. After waiting in line, the family members are instructed to remove any phones, tablets, or liquids from their carry-on luggage and put them into trays. Only small bottles of liquids, creams, or gels—such as toothpaste or shampoo—are allowed in the carry-on bags. They have to be put in special see-through plastic bags.

Sofia, Rohan, and their parents put the trays next to their carry-on luggage on the conveyor belt, which is slowly gobbled up by the X-ray machine. Security agent Francine looks at the X-ray pictures, which reveal what's inside the bags as if by magic. Next, security agent Malu tells everyone to walk through the metal detector.

The X-ray machine scans every bag.

BEEP-BEEP-BEEP! the machine rings out as Scott, Sofia and Rohan's dad, walks through. "Please hold your arms out, sir," says agent Hector politely as he waves a scanner over Scott's body. It turns out his metal belt set off the machine! Scott takes it off and goes through the metal detector again. This time there is no beep, and he is waved through by Hector.

Uh oh! Further down the line Akari forgot to take out a big bottle of water from her suitcase. Francine sees the bottle in the X-ray picture of Akari's bag. Akari has to give the bottle to another agent, who puts it into a recycling bin. "I'll remember next time!" says Akari with a shake of her head.

The security scanner

At security, you might be asked to walk through a scanner. These machines check for anything that may be hidden in your pockets to make sure nobody is taking forbidden items onto the plane. But don't worry if the machine makes a noise on your turn. They are designed to detect small metals, so even a pin or a watch you've forgotten to take off can make it go *BEEP-BEEP*!

Body scanner

While you stand very still, the machine scans your body and shows the security agent a picture that looks kind of like a cartoon person. If it detects any metals, a circle pops up letting the agent know where it is.

Pat down

Sometimes security agents need to check for anything hidden under passengers' clothes. They will ask you to hold out your arms while they gently pat your clothes.

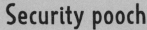

Metal detector wand

Security agents will sometimes wave a metal detector wand over passengers. It will beep if any metals are detected.

Security pooch

Dogs have very sensitive noses, so some airports have specially trained dogs (known as K-9s, as in "canines"!) whose job is to sniff passengers' luggage. They can smell items that aren't allowed on planes.

The swab is usually attached to a long stick.

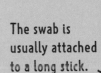

The machine puffs air through the cloth swab and "sniffs" it.

Swab machine

Agents sometimes wipe fabric swabs on your hands, clothes, and luggage. The swabs are then scanned by a machine that will tell agents if everything is safe to go on the plane.

What do airports look like?

Airports come in all shapes and sizes. Some are small, with just one terminal building where people get on and off planes, and one runway where planes take off and land. Some airports are huge, with multiple runways and many different terminals.

Fire station

Every airport has a fire station in case of an emergency. Firefighters are always on duty.

Runways and taxiways

Airplanes take off and land on long runways that are specially built to handle their weight. They can go either way down the runway—it depends on which way the wind is blowing.

A wind sock shows which way the wind is blowing.

Main terminal

Passengers arrive by car, bus, or train at the main terminal. They check in, go through security, and then find the gate where their plane is parked.

DEPARTURES

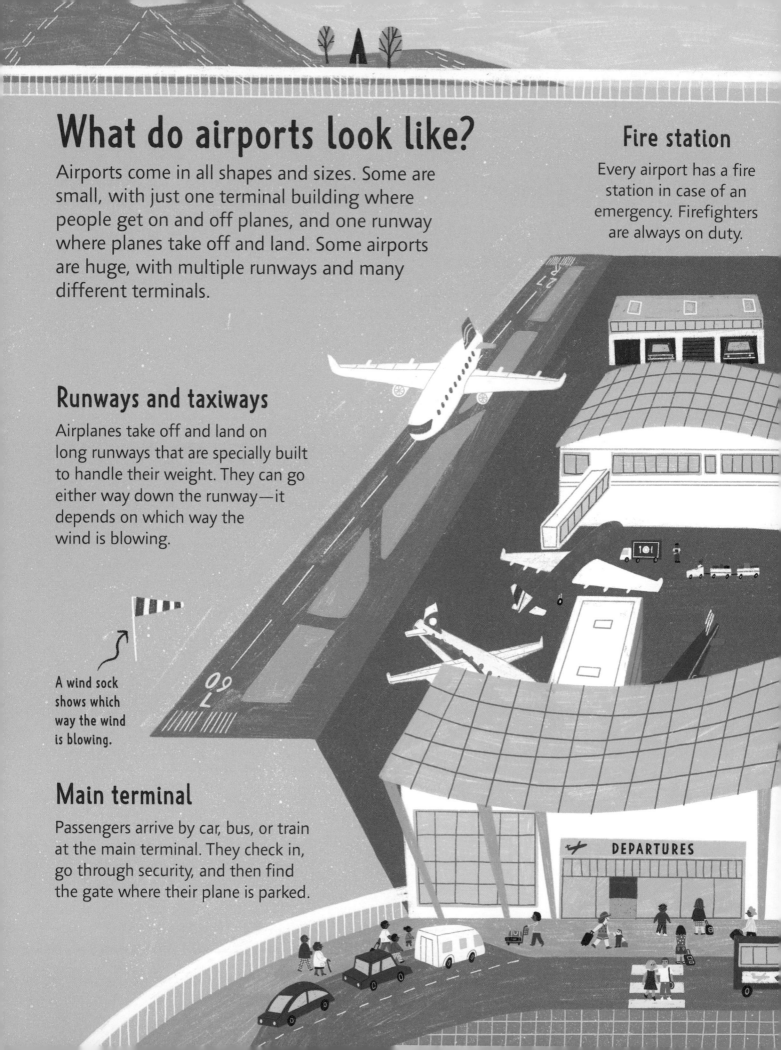

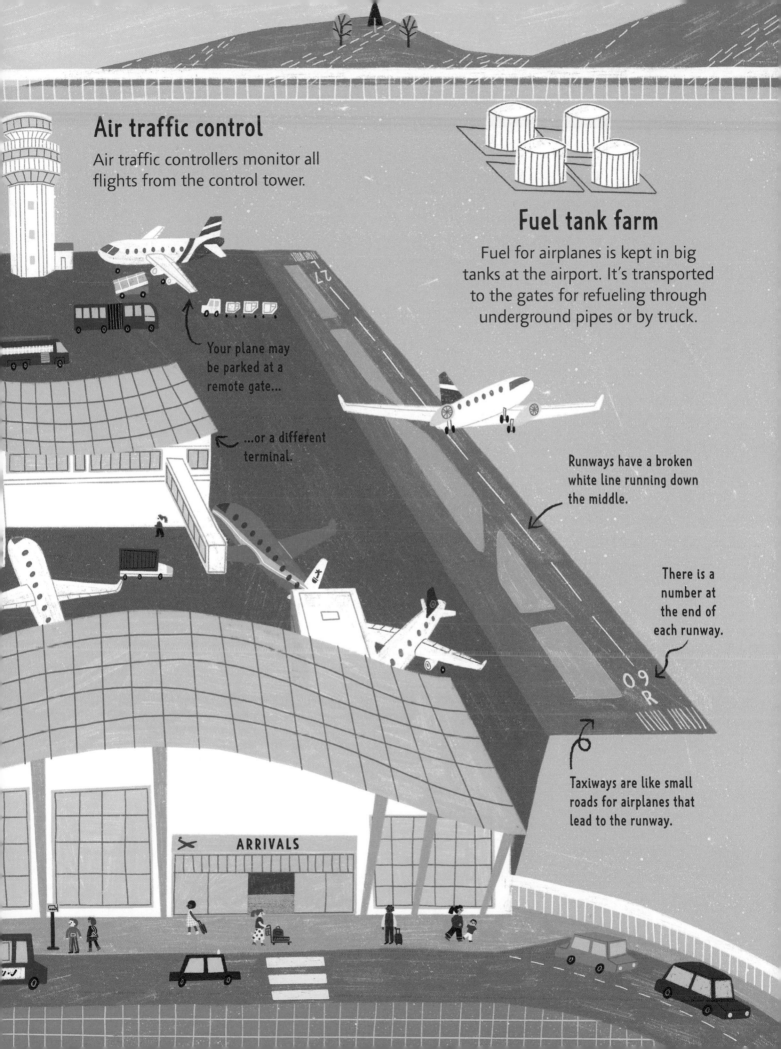

Air traffic control

Air traffic controllers monitor all flights from the control tower.

Your plane may be parked at a remote gate...

...or a different terminal.

Fuel tank farm

Fuel for airplanes is kept in big tanks at the airport. It's transported to the gates for refueling through underground pipes or by truck.

Runways have a broken white line running down the middle.

There is a number at the end of each runway.

Taxiways are like small roads for airplanes that lead to the runway.

ARRIVALS

The departures lounge

After going through security, Priya looks for her flight on the departures board. This is a big screen that tells everyone at which gate their plane is parked and when it is time to board. Priya's flight is at Gate 9, so she makes her way through the departures lounge to get there.

In the departures lounge there are lots of stores selling all sorts of food and drinks, souvenirs, and things you might want to buy for your flight, such as earplugs and magazines. Melinda munches on a delicious chocolate muffin that her papa bought for her, while her daddy drinks his coffee. Papa keeps an eye on the departures board so that they know when to go to their gate. They don't board for another hour, so they can sit back and relax!

Meanwhile, Chantelle is waiting for an overnight flight to Johannesburg, in South Africa, where she has an important meeting to attend. Her company wants her to be wide awake and ready for the day when she arrives, so they are paying extra for her to fly in business class. Business-class seats on the airplane turn into beds so she can get a good night's sleep.

Chantelle works on her laptop in the business-class lounge. This is a quiet and comfortable place where people flying in business class can work, relax, and have some food. Chantelle sips on some tea while she waits for her flight.

The baggage system

Underneath the terminal, the luggage that's been checked in goes on an exciting journey before it even gets to the airplane! Suitcases travel through a hidden maze of trays, conveyor belts, chutes, and scanners. Every piece of luggage is first scanned to make sure nothing dangerous or forbidden is inside. Things such as fireworks and matches aren't allowed on airplanes for safety reasons.

Each item of luggage is tipped into a tray.

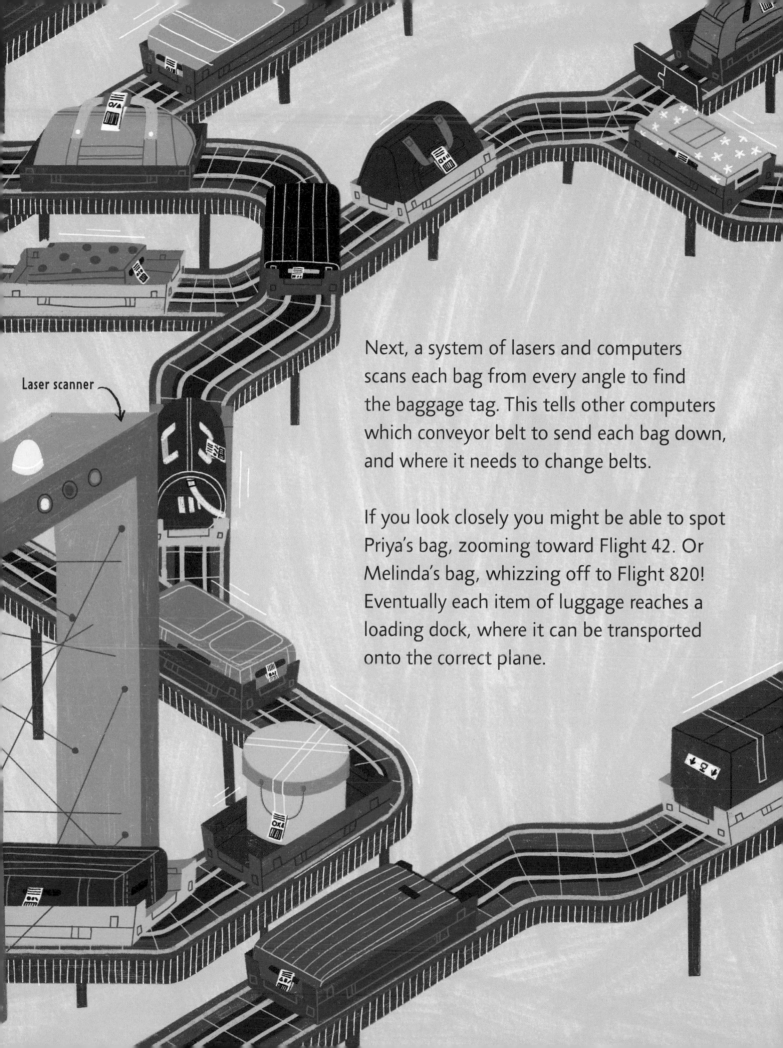

Laser scanner

Next, a system of lasers and computers scans each bag from every angle to find the baggage tag. This tells other computers which conveyor belt to send each bag down, and where it needs to change belts.

If you look closely you might be able to spot Priya's bag, zooming toward Flight 42. Or Melinda's bag, whizzing off to Flight 820! Eventually each item of luggage reaches a loading dock, where it can be transported onto the correct plane.

Loading luggage

Whoosh! There goes Priya's bag, zooming down the chute to the baggage loading dock. This is where the bags are collected before being taken to the airplanes. Baggage loaders Benjamin, Courtney, and Jamal check the bags and load them onto baggage trucks. They need to be very organized—no one likes lost luggage!

On some bigger planes, bags are put into big metal containers that are then loaded onto the plane. That makes everything faster when there are lots of bags, and it means the airline can fit more luggage and other cargo onto the plane. The baggage loaders wait for all the bags to arrive before driving the fully loaded trucks over to where the airplane is waiting by its gate.

In a matter of minutes, the bags reach Bob, Chad, and Simone who are inside the hold of the airplane—underneath where the passengers sit. Bob is at the top of the baggage loader conveyor waiting for the bags to come up. He then passes them on to Chad and Simone who stack the bags on top of one another. It's a team effort.

Baggage loading usually happens at the same time as the passengers are boarding the plane. So next time you grab a seat with a view, look out the window to see if you can spot your bag as it goes up the baggage loader conveyor!

A bird's-eye view

The air traffic control tower sits high above the airport. Inside, air traffic controllers can see everything! Their job is to monitor all incoming and outgoing airplanes to make sure that everything is running smoothly.

Through their headsets they can communicate with any pilot, anywhere. There is no time for gossip though—communication needs to be kept to a minimum in case a pilot is in trouble and needs urgent advice.

Trixie and her team are prepared to handle any type of emergency, but so far their day is going very smoothly. Trixie is handling arrivals. She tells the pilots of approaching planes which runway to land on and which direction the wind is coming from. She also checks that their planes are far enough away from the planes in front of and behind them.

Trixie's colleague Ross is handling departures. He watches Flight 47 take off before he tells the next plane to get in the line at the far end of the runway.

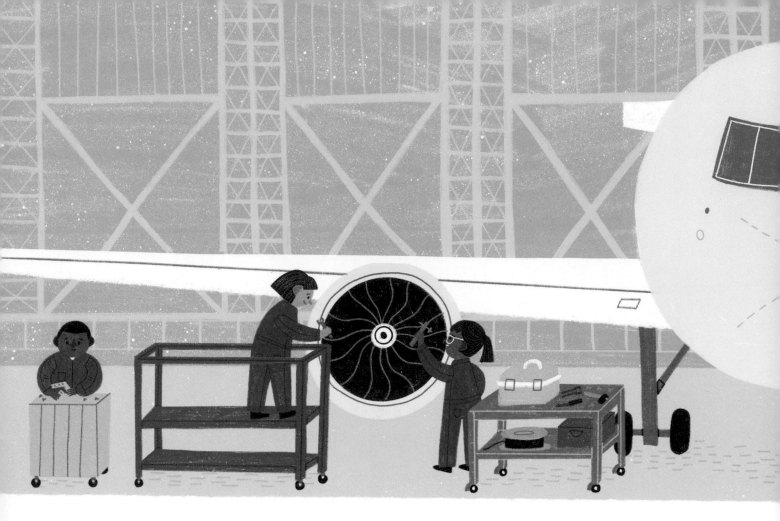

The repair shop

No matter how big or small they are, airplanes are complicated machines made up of millions (yes, millions!) of parts. Maintenance engineers make sure that these parts are all working correctly so the planes can fly safely. They check planes before and after every flight, and every couple of months they tow planes into a big building called a hangar for a day or so for extra checks. A hangar is like a repair shop, but for airplanes!

Maintenance engineers are mechanics for airplanes. They use all kinds of tools, from hammers and screwdrivers to tablet computers and high-tech scanners. They are extremely skilled and know how to fix all sorts of problems.

Jasmine and Mia discover that one of the engines on this airplane needs to be repaired. So that the plane can keep flying, they need to put a new engine on while they repair the old one.

Mia opens up the outside cover, which is called a cowling, and she and Jasmine lower the old engine onto a cart with wheels. Bradley rolls up a new engine and helps them raise it into place. A few more tweaks and checks, and this plane is ready to fly again!

The planes you'll see

All kinds of different planes land at the airport. Some carry only one person, while others can carry up to 853 passengers! Usually, the bigger the plane, the farther it can fly. If you visit an airport, which is the biggest plane you can find?

Newer planes have winglets at the end of the wings. These help save fuel, allowing the plane to fly farther.

Turboprops

Turboprops carry around 50 to 70 people on flights of about an hour. You can spot them because of their propeller engines.

Regional jets

With small jet engines at the back of the plane, regional jets carry around 50 to 70 passengers on short-haul flights, usually a couple of hours long.

Business jets

Some business executives and celebrities fly in small business jets. These are private airplanes, rather than planes used by airlines.

Narrow-body plane

Most airplanes you'll spot at the airport will be narrow-body aircraft. They come in different colors, depending on which airline they belong to. These medium-sized planes carry around 150 to 200 people.

Double-deckers

The biggest kind of plane is a double-decker. They are two stories high and can carry more than 850 passengers!

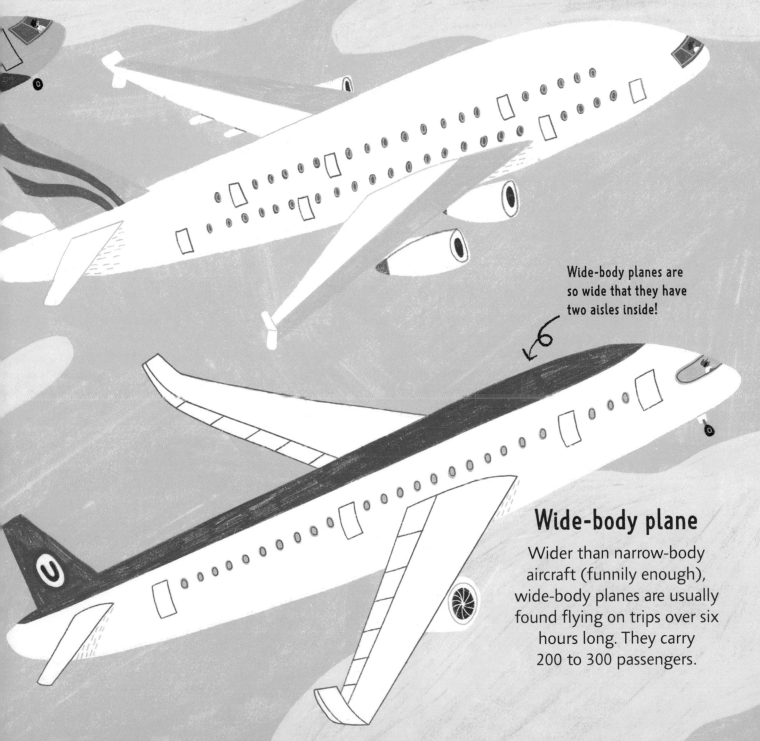

Wide-body planes are so wide that they have two aisles inside!

Wide-body plane

Wider than narrow-body aircraft (funnily enough), wide-body planes are usually found flying on trips over six hours long. They carry 200 to 300 passengers.

A team of chefs

Have you ever wondered where the food you eat on an airplane comes from? It's all made by talented chefs inside a huge kitchen at the airport. Everyone has their own job to do, and every delicious and healthy meal is the result of a long assembly line where everyone helps out.

Today, Safir is in charge of the vegetables, so she adds broccoli to every meal. Can you find Safir? She's wearing a white hairnet and blue apron—but, oh! That's not very helpful, so is everyone else! The staff in the kitchen wear these special uniforms to make sure the kitchen is kept clean. Not far from Safir is Alexandra, who is working on desserts. She's adding a piece of juicy watermelon to every fruit plate that goes past. Quick, Alexandra, don't miss that one!

Every meal is carefully cooked, chilled, placed onto trays, and loaded into carts. These carts then roll into special trucks that lift them up to your plane. When it's mealtime up in the air, flight attendants roll the carts down the airplane aisles for you to have your pick.

Before loading the carts, Cory checks that everything is on the tray. Main meal, bread and butter, cutlery—it's all in there! These meals will feed a lot of very hungry passengers today.

Jetways and airstairs

When an airplane is parked at a gate, airfield engineers use moving bridges on wheels called jetways, or airbridges, to make sure that everyone gets on and off safely. At Gate 5, Captain Flora guides her plane in while Ravi waits at the jetway's controls. Once Flora has stopped the plane and turned off the engine, Ravi uses a joystick to move the jetway to the plane. Once all of the passengers have gotten off the plane, the craft will be prepped for its next flight!

Jetways have a special bendy seal at the top so passengers don't get wet if it's raining.

Only authorized staff can drive airstairs trucks.

When an airplane is parked on a remote stand far away from the terminal, airfield engineers like Carl and Mosadi make sure that everyone gets on and off the plane. Carl drives an airstairs truck and carefully parks it underneath the doors of the airplane, waiting for new passengers to arrive.

When the shuttle bus carrying the passengers reaches the remote stand, Carl waves to them to wait in the bus until the crew are ready for them to climb the stairs with their luggage. Mosadi greets flight attendant Patrick with a cheery "Hello!"

"Stop!" Mosadi calls to passengers Moira and Heather. They aren't looking where they are going and nearly walk underneath the wing, where the engine is. Mosadi carefully guides them around the wing toward the rear door.

At the boarding gate

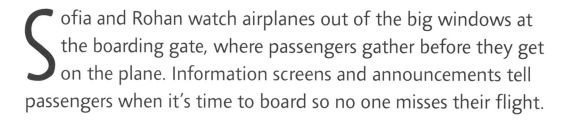

Sofia and Rohan watch airplanes out of the big windows at the boarding gate, where passengers gather before they get on the plane. Information screens and announcements tell passengers when it's time to board so no one misses their flight.

Sometimes you can even see the pilots. Rohan points them out to his sister. "Give them a big wave, Sofia," he says. "They might wave back!"

Cindy and Tamika are boarding-gate agents. They use a computer to make sure that everyone is on the right plane. Tamika makes an announcement calling all preboarding passengers to the gate. These are people who might need a little more time or assistance to board. Among the group are Priya, who needs to transfer to the special airplane wheelchair; Dan, who wants some time to get baby Jack settled; and Mrs. Sheffield, who uses a cane. It's almost time for takeoff!

Ramp supervisor
Kay makes sure the airplane is ready to go and that everyone has performed their jobs.

Baggage handlers
Sarah and Richard drive luggage from the terminal to the plane and make sure it gets on board.

Catering staff
Tim and Jayda work for the catering company, which makes all the food that passengers and crew eat on board.

Preparing for takeoff

Lots of different people have important jobs to do before an airplane is ready to take to the sky. For safety, passengers normally get on and off the plane on its left-hand side. All the jobs—such as catering, refueling, and baggage loading—usually happen on the right-hand side.

Food delivery

Tim drives a truck called a scissor lift that carries all the meal carts prepared by the catering team. Jayda rolls every cart straight into the airplane!

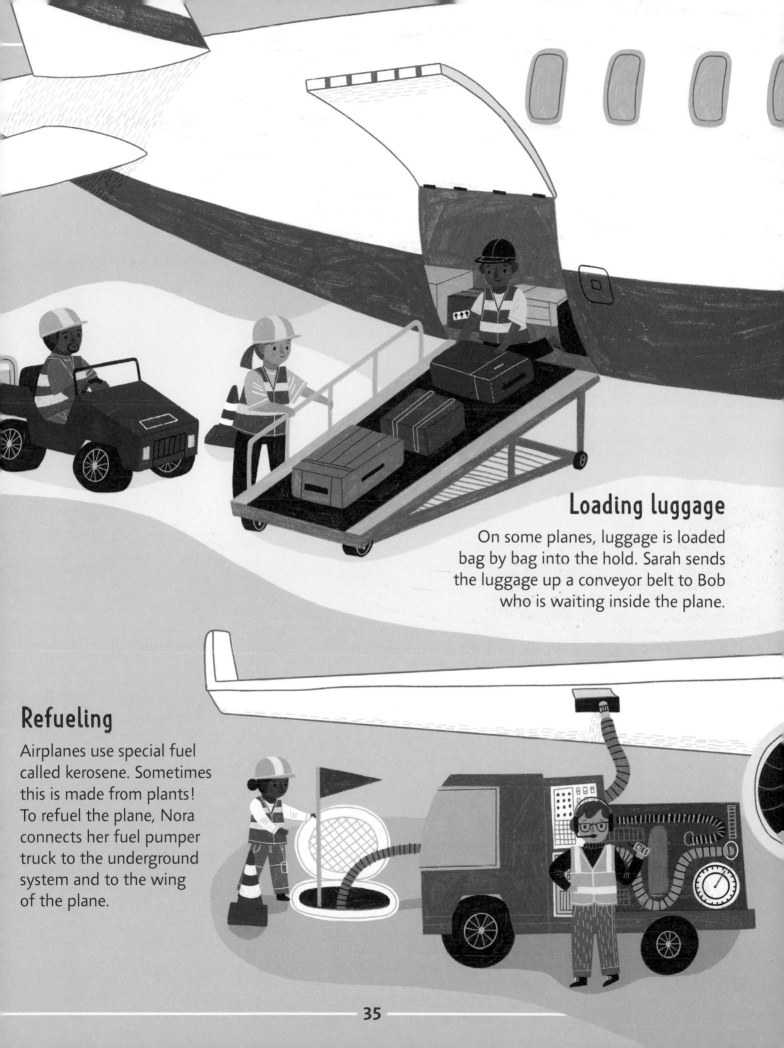

Loading luggage

On some planes, luggage is loaded bag by bag into the hold. Sarah sends the luggage up a conveyor belt to Bob who is waiting inside the plane.

Refueling

Airplanes use special fuel called kerosene. Sometimes this is made from plants! To refuel the plane, Nora connects her fuel pumper truck to the underground system and to the wing of the plane.

In the belly of the plane

Everything that an airplane carries in its baggage hold is called cargo. This includes suitcases, lifesaving medicine, and even fresh fish! On big planes, luggage is loaded into specially shaped metal containers that fit inside the curved body of the aircraft. Some other cargo goes in these containers too, while some is loaded onto flat pallets.

Did someone order sushi? Roger and his team are handling a big shipment of fresh fish. Roger is a loadmaster, and he is responsible for making sure everything is loaded in the right order and safely secured in the hold. One of the team, Mahmoud, checks his tablet to see which pallet to load next. Before arriving here at the loading dock, the fish was put into containers in a large warehouse at the airport. A refrigerated room kept the fish cold!

Some containers are giant fridges that keep cargo like fresh fish or medicine cold.

Loadmasters use tablets to keep track of what has been loaded on the plane.

Weird and wonderful cargo

Airplanes can transport all kinds of special cargo in the hold. Have you ever wondered what might be underneath your seat while you doze off to sleep up in the cabin?

Flying animals?

If you think it's only people that fly around the world, think again. Some animals have busy schedules too! Racehorses need to travel to international races, while animals such as pandas are flown to zoos in different countries.

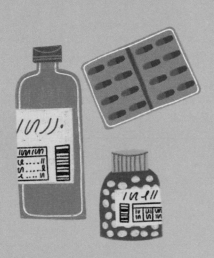

Medicines

Vaccines and other medicines can be flown from where they are made to where they are needed. They often have to be kept in refrigerated containers.

Open wide

Some planes are specially made to carry cargo. A few of these special planes even have noses that lift up to allow the cargo on board. It almost looks like the plane is smiling!

Fresh flowers are jetted all over the world.

Fresh food

Have you ever wondered how bananas, mangoes, and other tropical fruit can be bought in shops across the globe all year round? Fresh fruit and vegetables are flown to international destinations daily.

Before they fly, animals traveling on planes are examined by vets to make sure they are healthy.

Flashy cars

Sports cars or luxury vehicles can be delivered from the factory to their new owners by plane. They're carefully loaded on board using special equipment.

Wildlife at the airport

Felix the falcon swoops around the airport chasing away geese. He has a very important job: making sure that birds don't fly too close to airplanes. His trainer Meena wears a special leather glove for him to land on, and she gives him a treat. "Good job, Felix. All that training paid off!"

While Meena deals with the birds, Ken is busy taking care of bigger wildlife. Today, two deer are getting too close to the fence that surrounds the airport. For everyone's safety, they shouldn't be here.

Ken drives his truck up to them and turns on the speakers. *Oonk! Oonk!* He plays a recording of a deer danger call, and the deer run back to the forest. They might visit the airport again, but Ken will be ready!

Is that a bird? Is it a plane? No, it's a drone! Sometimes, if falcons like Felix aren't available, airports use drones to buzz around and scare off birds. Airplanes are the only things with wings allowed at the airport! If birds fly into an airplane or its engines, they could cause an accident, so it's always better to be on the safe side!

Firefighters at the ready!

Did you know that every airport has a fire station? Although accidents and fires are very rare, firefighters need to be ready for every emergency. Liam is the fire chief, and he's supervising firefighters Judith and Caillou as they check that all the hoses, fire engines, and other equipment are ready for whatever may come their way.

Firefighters at the airport use special fire engines that can go off-road if needed. That's so that they can drive over the grassy areas around runways in case an airplane skids off while taking off or landing.

The fire engines that Judith and Caillou drive have big nozzles on the front that can spray foam or water, depending on what's needed to fight the fire. Occasionally when they have some downtime, firefighters spray water in a big arch to welcome new planes to the airport!

Firefighters train regularly to put out fires as quickly and safely as possible. Today Judith and Caillou are performing a routine fire drill. They are using training equipment that includes something that looks like an airplane... but isn't! This fake airplane is called a fire training rig, and it's used by firefighters to learn how to put out an aircraft fire. Liam shows Caillou and Judith where to aim. "Lower, Caillou, by the engine!"

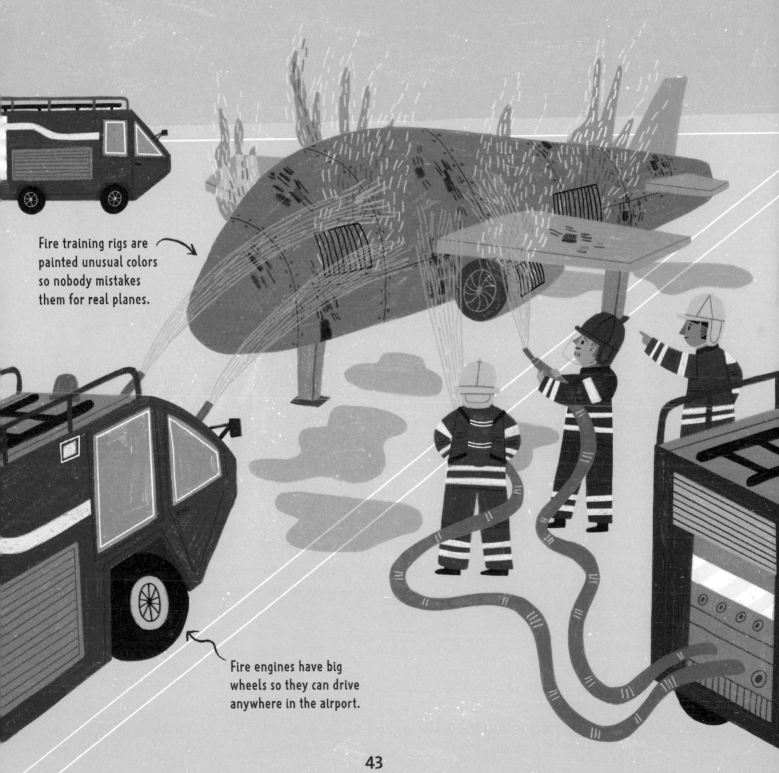

Fire training rigs are painted unusual colors so nobody mistakes them for real planes.

Fire engines have big wheels so they can drive anywhere in the airport.

Pilots and flight attendants

Every airplane has at least two pilots and a team of flight attendants who make up its crew. They work together to fly the plane and look after the passengers. Make sure to greet them when you board the plane!

Pre-flight prep

Before every flight, the crew have a meeting to get to know one another and share information about the flight time, passengers, and safety protocols.

The team

Pilots and flight attendants walk through the airport and go through security and passport control—just like you! Captain Beverly is in charge of this crew today.

Checklists help pilots make sure they don't forget anything.

Every airline has a different uniform. How many can you spot in this book?

Flight deck checklist

On board, Captain Beverly and First Officer Jean-Luc take their seats in the flight deck, the cabin where all the controls are. Before every flight, they use a checklist to make sure that the plane is ready to fly. "Parking brake?" "Set!" "Chocks?" "Removed!"

Safety first

Flight attendants keep all the passengers on the plane safe. Before taking off, Fintan, Shawna, and Liza check that all of the safety equipment is on board and ready to be used if needed.

Getting on the plane

Once inside the plane, Sofia and Rohan look at their tickets with a confused look on their faces. "20C and 20E, what does that mean?" Their mom shows flight attendant Shawna the family's tickets. "Just walk down the aisle until you see the number 20 above the seats," Shawna says cheerfully.

On an airplane, every seat has a row number and a letter on it. Row 1 is at the front, followed by row 2, all the way back until you run out of plane! The letters start with A on the left side of the plane, and then follow the alphabet across the seats to the right.

There are three seats in every row on their plane. Rohan sits in a middle seat next to his mom in one row, while Sofia sits next to the aisle on the other side of the aisle. Rohan looks at the other passengers still boarding and wonders where they've come from.

Sofia and Rohan want to read their books during the flight, so they put their backpacks underneath the seats in front of them. Their parents plan on taking a long nap as soon as the plane takes off, so they lift their bags into the overhead bins so they're out of the way.

Once everyone has taken their seats, it's time for the safety demonstration. Flight attendant Zion shows all the passengers how the crew keep them safe on board.

After pointing to the nearest emergency exits, Zion demonstrates how to use the seat belts. The airplane seat belt is different from car seat belts, so Rohan has to practice a couple of times. "There you go, Rohan. You've got it!" says his mom.

Up in the clouds

Just like Sofia and Rohan, Melinda and her dads have just boarded their plane. Once the doors are closed, the airplane is ready to go! When an aeroplane moves on the ground it's called *taxiing*.

Melinda, who was at first nervous for her trip, is now excited to see the world from the sky. She watches out the window as the airplane taxis past the air traffic control tower and the fire station.

"Cabin crew, ready for takeoff," says Captain Sally over the loudspeaker.

The engines start to spin really fast and make a loud noise, and the plane accelerates forward. They whizz down the runway and then up, up, up they go! Melinda is pushed back into her seat. It's just like being on a ride. Their airplane makes a big turn after it takes off, and Melinda spots the airport. "Look, Daddy, there it is!"

After the airplane finishes climbing, it levels off at what is called the cruising altitude, usually around 35,000 ft (11,000 m) up in the sky. Everyone settles down for the flight, but first it's time for dinner. Flight attendant Natalie rolls the cart down the aisle. "Chicken or pasta, which would you prefer?" Natalie then hands the passengers their meals on one of the trays that was carefully prepared earlier by the catering team.

Prepare for landing

On a different flight, Captain Monica and her crew are about to land at our airport after a long journey. Flight attendant Roxanne walks through the plane reminding anyone who has reclined their seats to put them back upright and to put away all the tray tables. She also makes sure everyone's seat belts are fastened and that all bags have been put away, either into the overhead bins or underneath the seats in front of each passenger.

In the flight deck, Captain Monica and First Officer Akin concentrate on landing the plane. They're using all of their skill and experience to fly the airplane smoothly, lower and lower, toward the airport. Air traffic controllers tell them which direction to fly in and when to make turns so the plane lines up with the correct runway. In the distance, they spot the runway lights, which help them judge how far away the airport is and how high they're flying.

Just before landing, an automatic system called a radio altimeter calls out how high they are in feet: "Fifty... forty... thirty... twenty...". As they cross the near end of the runway, they reduce power on the engines, and the airplane floats to the ground with a little bump. Time for the brakes, and here we are! Good job, team!

Passport control

When you fly to a different country, you have to pass through a checkpoint, which is called passport control. This is where immigration officers make sure everyone is who they say they are. The airport is very busy today! There's a line of recently landed passengers that zigzags all the way down the immigration hall, just like a huge worm.

At the checkpoint, you either show your passport to an immigration officer or use an electronic gate that scans your passport. May has just arrived from Lagos, in Nigeria. She's incredibly tired but happy to have arrived. She hands her passport to Kevin, an immigration officer. Kevin checks every passenger's passport, looks it up in the computer system, and sometimes asks questions about their trip. Once he's happy he stamps their passport and waves them through.

Naoki just arrived from Tokyo, in Japan. He uses the electronic gate, where the line is a lot shorter. He holds the photo page of his passport on the scanner and looks into the automatic camera. A picture appears on the screen, and numbers count down: 3, 2, 1... flash! The gate uses facial recognition technology to scan this picture and confirm it is Naoki.

Success! The screen shows Naoki a green arrow. The gate opens, and he walks through to go find his luggage.

Where's my bag?

id you check a large bag before your flight? If you did, it will reappear on the baggage claim carousel belt, usually about 30 minutes or so after your plane pulls up to the gate. You can't see them, but baggage loaders are working as quickly as they can to unload your bags from the plane, drive them to the terminal, and put them on the right carousel belt where everyone is waiting for their bags. The carousel belts slowly wind around and around so everyone can get their luggage.

Matilda just arrived from a beach vacation. She's not prepared for the cold weather here and quickly looks for a sweater. She still needs to pick up her surfboard! People check all sorts of luggage. Can you help Matilda find her surfboard?

Oh no. Murphy's suitcase didn't arrive! Sometimes luggage gets left behind at the departure airport. Murphy goes to the lost luggage desk, where Peter asks him some questions: What color is it? How big is it? Does it have wheels, and if so, how many?

Peter puts all this information into the computer, and luckily he finds Murphy's bag. Peter apologizes and requests for it to be put on the next flight. Murphy's bag will then be delivered straight to his hotel.

Reuniting with friends and family

Once you pass through the final doors to the arrivals area, your journey through the airport is complete. Here, family and friends might be waiting to welcome you. Is that someone's dad waiting with flowers? Can you spot the driver ready to take the businesswoman to her important meeting? Oh, look, that family has just reunited after a long time!

In the arrivals area you'll also find all sorts of ways to continue on your journey even if someone hasn't come to collect you. Perhaps there's a train you need to rush to, or maybe you'll take the bus to reach some friends in the city.

Wait... is that... you know... that famous actor? From that blockbuster movie? All kinds of people fly through the airport, and sometimes that includes big stars. Did you see anybody famous on your trip? "No pictures, please," says the actor's bodyguard as they make their way past the paparazzi.

Nighttime at the airport

At most airports, there aren't many flights taking off or landing late at night, but the airport never goes to sleep. With fewer flights, there are fewer people needed to send them where they need to go. Air traffic controller Trixie waves good night to her colleagues who have arrived for their night shifts.

Other parts of the airport are still buzzing with activity. In the maintenance hangar, planes are being checked and repaired. At the gates, mechanics and technicians check that every seat belt and in-flight movie screen is working properly. On every airplane, cleaners replace things such as pillows and blankets, ready for the first flights in the morning.

In the terminal, Javier closes up a café for the night. In just a few hours, eager passengers will be lining up for their morning coffees. Oliver cleans up a mess on the floor so nobody slips on it, while security guard Janusz patrols the halls. And waving good night to their colleagues, pilots Monica and Akin head home for the night.

Outside, it gets quieter and quieter. The airport is waiting for tomorrow when new passengers will arrive to start a brand-new day.

Glossary

Airline
A company that runs flights and employs pilots, flight attendants, and staff on the ground.

Air traffic controller
A person who directs airplanes onto and off the runways at the airport, and into the air!

Cabin crew
The people who look after you on board a flight and serve you meals and drinks. Also known as flight attendants.

Cargo
Any sort of goods or packages being sent by air—from smartphones to elephants!

Check-in
A special desk where you get your boarding pass and drop off your luggage.

Cruising altitude
The height above the earth at which airplanes stay for most of their flight.

Drone
A flying machine of any size that doesn't have a pilot on board.

Engine
A big motor that spins really fast and propels an airplane through the air.

Flight deck
The special area at the front of an airplane where the pilots sit. It has controls and screens that tell them where the plane is and how it's flying.

Hangar
A big building in the airport where airplanes are repaired.

Hold
The space inside the airplane, underneath the cabin floor, where all the luggage and cargo are stored.

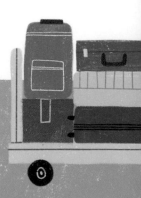

Immigration officer

A person employed by the government who checks your passport when you arrive in a new country.

Jetway

A movable walkway that connects to an airplane. Also known as an airbridge.

Loadmaster

A person in charge of making sure that all the cargo on a plane is secured properly.

Maintenance engineer

The airplane version of a mechanic, who keeps planes in tip-top condition and repairs anything that goes wrong.

Pilot

A person who flies airplanes.

Radio altimeter

A piece of equipment that shows pilots how high an airplane is flying.

Runway

The long tarmac road at an airport where airplanes take off and land.

Taxiing

When planes move around the airport on their wheels, it is called taxiing. Just like a taxi you might ride in!

Terminal

The big building at an airport where you check in, drop your bags, and get on a plane. You will get off your plane at a terminal at your destination.

X-ray machine

A machine that uses X-ray waves to see inside luggage and make sure nobody is taking anything dangerous on board a plane.

Index

This has been a

NEON ◆ SQUID

production

For my parents, who gave me a love for the world we live in, and for Fintan, who makes my heart fly.

Author: John Walton

Illustrator: Hannah Abbo

Editorial Assistant: Malu Rocha
US Editor: Allison Singer Kushnir
Proofreader: Laura Gilbert
Indexer: Elizabeth Wise

Copyright © 2023 St. Martin's Press
120 Broadway, New York, NY 10271

Created for St. Martin's Press
by Neon Squid
The Stables, 4 Crinan Street,
London, N1 9XW

EU representative: Macmillan
Publishers Ireland Ltd,
1st Floor, The Liffey Trust Centre,
117–126 Sheriff Street Upper,
Dublin 1, D01 YC43

10 9 8 7 6 5 4 3 2 1

Library of Congress Cataloging-in-
Publication Data is available.

Printed and bound in Guangdong,
China by Leo Paper Products Ltd.

ISBN: 978-1-684-49309-8

Published in July 2023.

www.neonsquidbooks.com